Profile 19 – JACK DONOVAN

Published as part of Gandon Editions' PROFILES series on Irish artists (details, page 82).

ISBN 0946846 200

© Gandon Editions, LCGA and the artist, 2004.
All rights reserved.

Editor   John O'Regan

Asst Editor   Nicola Dearey
Design   John O'Regan
                (© Gandon Editions, 2004)
Production   Nicola Dearey
                Gunther Berkus
Photography   Con Kelleher
Printing   Nicholson & Bass, Belfast

Distributed by Gandon and its overseas agents

GANDON EDITIONS
Oysterhaven, Kinsale, Co Cork, Ireland

tel   +353 (0)21-4770830
fax   +353 (0)21-4770755
e-mail   gandon@eircom.net
web-site   www.gandon-editions.com

cover   *After Velázquez*, 1978 (detail)
back cover   *Susannah and the Elders*,
                1975-76

Gandon Editions is grant-aided by
The Arts Council /
An Chomhairle Ealaíon

JACK DONOVAN
RETROSPECTIVE OF PAINTINGS, 1959-2004

Published by Limerick City Gallery of Art, in association with Gandon Editions, to coincide with the exhibition of the same name at LCGA (11 September – 23 October, 2004).

ISBN 09544291 33 clothbound edition

LIMERICK CITY GALLERY OF ART
Pery Square, Limerick, Ireland

tel   +353 (0)61-310633
fax   +353 (0)61-310228
e-mail   lcgartzz@iol.ie
web-site   www.limerickcity.ie/LCGA

Director   Mike Fitzpatrick

LCGA acknowledgements

Publication and exhibition grant-aided by The Arts Council, and supported by Tim Donovan and Clem Lyons

Part of the exhibition will tour to the West Cork Arts Centre, Skibbereen (February 2005), and Draíocht Arts Centre, Blanchardstown (March).

contents

LCGA
LIMERICK CITY
GALLERY OF ART

Profile

Jack Donovan

GANDON EDITIONS

Jack Donovan's Dark Simplicities

GERRY DUKES

Balcony Series (with self-portrait)
1978, oil and collage on board, 75 x 70 cm

IT WAS NOT UNTIL I BECAME A CASUAL TEACHER OF ART HISTORY IN THAT GRIM BUILDING OPPOSITE the even grimmer prison on Mulgrave Street that I first encountered Jack Donovan. This is only partially true – I had seen a few of his paintings before first meeting with the man himself. These were casually distributed in odd places around the art school, some on view, others with their faces turned modestly to the walls. One in particular, lodged behind a chair in the staffroom, caught my attention. I found myself drawn to the room again and again, even when I had no business there.

The painting (paper collage and oil on board) is one of that lengthy *Balcony Series* for which Jack Donovan is rightly celebrated. Posed and poised behind a low parapet, right and left, are two female nudes (collaged cut-outs from pin-up magazines), one wearing a top hat and the other sporting a cloche affair. Seated centre is a deeply ambiguous male clerical figure with suffocated, dark features. From his right hand, languidly dangling over the parapet, depends a curious metallic bauble on a string; just to his left, hanging over the balcony, a badge of office or a club banner. Behind these three figures, a fourth is emerging from interior darkness into the glaucous light of the painting. It is a bearded male with ruffed shirt and bow-tie, and is a pitiless self-portrait of the artist.

Boning up, as I was at the time, on the history of the major European traditions in painting (it was my first gig as an art historian), I caught the references to Goya, Velázquez and Manet. But parody and pastiche were a long way from this arresting painting that I kept visiting and revisiting. The proprietorial gaze in Manet's great painting – the central male figure surveying and possessing the two gorgeously dressed women, one to his right and the other to his left – was comprehensively altered by the presence of two undressed women, seemingly ignored by the centrally posed male and by the representation of the painter himself as a witness or participant in whatever action was being recorded, performed or enacted. The 'balcony' paintings of Velázquez and Manet had undergone a paradigm shift, their paternalistic gender politics being deconstructed and displaced by a different order of representation and of reality. In a word or two, this was an Irish painting, demanding a response far different from those securely validated by the accepted canons of art history.

In a move of stunning simplicity, Donovan energised his painting with a few deft strokes used to blank out or black out the eyes of the figures. The effect of these strokes is to intensify the ambiguity of the scene depicted, closing off the possibilities of easy, consoling or facile interpretations. The four figures are locked into a scene which is literally unspeakable – there are no words can fix that atmosphere of dull and lewd tedium, of perversity and menace, of display and mystery. Those empty eye-sockets betoken a world that has been drained of certainties and significance, of shared meaning and self-respect. There is no gaze here, proprietorial or otherwise, merely blind indifference and empty husks. This provocative and disturbing painting was produced by Donovan in Limerick in the early 1970s.

The main body of his extensive work seems to me to eschew the so-called subtleties of modelling and shading in favour of a commitment to direct expression, unmodulated colour and uncluttered composition, all of which are, nevertheless, fully consonant with the principal European traditions in painting. Bosch is there, as are Lautrec and Matisse. Donovan has never been interested in or committed to verisimilitude, or in the academic disciplines it imposes. His vision and spirit have always been too free, too anarchic to be overborne or trammelled by the weight of art history. Other Limerick painters who have had the luck to be tutored by Jack Donovan – John Shinnors, Henry Morgan, Brian McMahon, et al – all manifest his enabling influence in varying and liberated ways that are eloquent testimony to the complete absence of dogma in Donovan's painterly practice.

Jack Donovan is a true artist because he thinks and acts in paint. What we make of his paintings does not centrally concern him; his business is putting the marks on the canvas. The realm of interpretation he leaves to the spectator, content with the capacity of his paintings to speak for themselves. What they speak of – those great runs of clowns, funfairs and circuses – is happy innocence and simple enjoyment. But again and again the runs are disrupted by images in which innocence is compromised and abused, where the world of nostalgia is assailed by the world of bitter experience. In these disturbing paintings Donovan is never strident; the impassive hand and eye conjoin to record, *pace* Beckett, how it is on this bitch of an earth.

Gerry Dukes teaches at MIC, University of Limerick. His *Illustrated Lives: Samuel Beckett* was published by Penguin in 2001. At present he is engaged in a study of modernist Irish writing as MIC Research Fellow.

 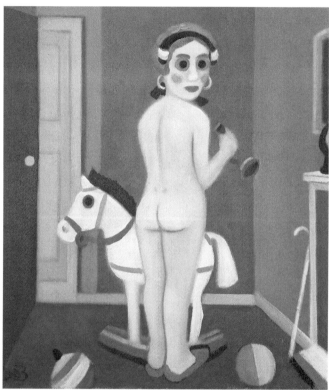

From Grouse Lodge to Pinkie Downey's – a Limerick drama

AIDAN DUNNE

Kilkee 1
1987, oil on canvas, 120 x 90 cm

opposite
The Nursery, Grouse Lodge
2003, oil on board, 90 x 78 cm
Nursery – Pinkie Downey series
2003, oil on board, 80 x 70 cm

OVER A PERIOD OF SEVERAL DECADES, JACK DONOVAN HAS DEVELOPED A PAINTERLY LANGUAGE that displays both remarkable consistency and restless inventiveness. In several ongoing, open-ended series of works, he has built up casts of characters and settings that, despite their obvious diversity, have become increasingly homogeneous in that they seem to reflect aspects of a single, sardonic world view. Jacobites and prostitutes, clerics and clowns, Shakespearean and Biblical characters, and fairground horses all inhabit what is, in essence, a common imaginative space. One could say that they all seem to be characters in the same farcical, tragicomic drama, a theatrical amalgam of the cruel and the absurd.

For the most part, the background in the paintings is as spare and stylised as a pared-down theatrical set. Part proscenium arch, part circus ring, it is a pictorial arena tailor-made to frame the double-take, the pratfall, the grandiloquent flourish. We, the audience, are cast in the role of voyeurs, but the performers, however extreme and ridiculous their situations, have a complicit knowingness that tells us they are in on the secret. A reciprocal relationship between seeing and being seen runs through the work. Various protagonists have their turn on the balcony, enjoying the spectacle below. Pink-fleshed nudes supervise offbeat *mise en scènes* with

7

the aplomb of seasoned conjurors' assistants. Many of the characters are caught up in dramatic vignettes suggesting folly and self-delusion, possessed by lust or zealotry, bound for hubristic ruin. There is a lot of humour, but also a very dark undercurrent.

Donovan bridles, reasonably enough, at any suggestion that he might be described as a Limerick artist. This resistance must relate to the idea that the city might, in some sense, define him, when he has made every effort to stand apart, when, indeed, he has always found himself instinctively opposed to its historically conservative character. He was, after all, schooled in a tradition that exalted academic values and looked to local painters, including Dermod O'Brien and Fergus Ryan, as fitting exemplars.

By nature, Donovan is and was from the start inclined towards a more open view of the Western tradition. What is true is that imagery derived from the region and its history, in the public and personal realm, is inextricably woven into his thematic concerns, providing him with an eclectic repertoire of narrative motifs that neatly summarise the human comedy. He is clearly fascinated by historical detail for this reason, not because it is symptomatic of uniqueness and a chauvinistic sense of place and identity, but because it typifies universal folly. In this regard, his introduction to the writings of Charles Darwin on evolution and natural selection, while he was in his teens, was pivotal in forming his perspective on Irish history and the nature and limitations of the human animal in general.

He lives in a part of the country steeped in history, and a great deal of his imagery derives from childhood memories. Both sides of his family had a strong sense of their own lineage. He listened to stories of Croom Castle at the time of the Jacobite rebellion, and was told that an ancestor had fought at the Boyne. There were suggestions that, much further back again, the family was perhaps Norse in origin and had held land in Limerick until driven out by the O'Briens and the Bourkes. The *Balcony series*, with a nod towards Manet, may well have been inspired by a familiar half-door at his grandmother's house that offered a truncated view of people going by. He visited Duffy's Circus and was brought to Shakespearean productions. During the summer he holidayed in the resort town of Kilkee – the beach-setting that recurs in the paintings. He did not, however, visit Pinkie Downey's – the renowned Limerick bordello had closed by the time he came to hear of it – but he was party to many accounts of it. The home of John Scanlon, the man who was executed in 1819 for murdering his wife Ellen Hanley, immortalised as Colleen Bawn by Gerald Griffin and Boucicault, is close by. Seán Ó Tuama, who presided over a poets' court at the Mungret Gate in the eighteenth century, is buried in Croom churchyard. Aspects of, and references to all of these things turn up in Donovan's work.

At a time when the nude was ostensibly corralled into an anodyne academic genre, Donovan caused a frisson of unease by using collaged fragments of photographs of women's bodies from porn magazines in his paintings, often with classical allusions. By amalgamating these mass-culture photographic fragments with elements of the high art tradition, he unmistakably re-sexualised the theme, or, perhaps more accurately, foregrounded the libidinous subtext implicit in the academic nude. This was provocative in more senses than one, not only in the context of a dominant, puritanical, conservative morality, but also, conversely, in terms of the representation of women. His fetishistic fragmentation of the female body, recognisably affiliated to Picasso's Cubist painting and De Kooning's aggressively deconstructed figures, could reasonably be interpreted in terms of the male gaze and the objectification of women's bodies.

Croom of the Merriment
1990/96, oil on canvas, 125 x 104 cm (detail)

Couple on balcony with balloon
2003-04, oil and collage on board, 81 x 66 cm (detail)

Nude, Pony and Clown
2004, oil on board, 84 x 80 cm (detail)

Even though he has largely dispensed with photographic collage, Donovan continues to depict women's bodies in a theatrically sexualised way. If pushed, one suspects that he would defend these representations partly on aesthetic grounds, but do they need defending? Certainly they are open to criticism, but at the same time they should be seen in the overall context of his view of life, history and society in terms of a crazy circus fuelled by the energy of errant and mischievous desire.

The space that he marks out in his paintings equates to the circus ring or the stage in the sense that it too is a space apart, a designated area in which the normal rules of reality are suspended, and in which reality can perhaps come under heightened scrutiny. Equally in the paintings, other emblematic settings, including the beach or the brothel, are viewed as stages on which human motivation and behaviour can be played out and anatomised. But as you view his work, it becomes evident that he also treats the classical illusionistic pictorial space of the Western tradition in the same way as a stage on which various generic dramas are enacted – religious and historical, the portrait and the still life. All are subsumed into his own personal theatre of paint, which is not to imply a dismissive attitude on his part towards the Western painting tradition. On the contrary, its obvious that he is carefully and respectfully attentive to it, and is, not least, a canny manipulator of colour and form.

Aidan Dunne is the art critic for *The Irish Times*, and has written extensively on Irish art.

The Accidental Teacher

INTERVIEW BY MIKE FITZPATRICK

Nude turning over
1962-63, oil on board, 122 x 122 cm

Jack Donovan
photographed by Con Kelleher, 2004

Mike Fitzpatrick – Can you recall your first encounter with art?

Jack Donovan – My mother had died when I was a couple of weeks old, so my father married another sister, my aunt. I assumed she was my mother until I was nine or ten, but that is another story. I was very fond of her – she and I were very close. We would come into town together, and I always remember my first visit to a gallery – it was Godwin's old gallery, alongside Todd's, the only commercial gallery in Limerick. We just walked in off the street. Thinking back now, I am pretty positive it was a Jack Yeats exhibition. I remember being puzzled at how they were painted and the weird colours used, and being excited about it but being mystified, because I reckoned I could draw better than that! I was about eight at the time.

What access did you have to other artworks?

Again I was lucky in the sense that although my father was the least intellectual man I knew – but a great sportsman, a great shot, he was the chemist in Rathkeale – he did, however, have a good selection of books and current magazines, and there were also a lot of books at my grandparents' place, Grouse Lodge, going back to the 1890s. When I was about twelve, I first saw Impressionist work. I became aware of it only after the war. You did not have the art magazines that you have now; and to get a colour reproduction was difficult. I remember getting a right buzz the first time I saw a Cézanne still life in colour in the 1950s.

In fairness, my parents knew I had a talent. The only art school they had heard of was the Slade, in London, which my father would have paid for. But someone mentioned you could do art in Limerick. There was no point staying on in school, as I knew one way or another that I was going to make my living out of painting. It was simple; there was nothing else I could do!

Can you recall your first experience at art school?

I think it was 1951. We came in on the Tralee train, and arrived into the original red-brick building, the 'Red Tech'. Dick Butcher, the previous headmaster, had just died. Originally from the north of England, he was a First World War veteran and he suffered from shell shock, poor man. He wasn't a painter, although he was a great craftsman, working in wood and metal.

It was still a school of the decorative arts.

Very much so. Anyway, poor old Butcher was being buried the morning we arrived. So we were met by Jim O'Donnell of the VEC [Vocational Education Committee]. I remember bringing a bundle of drawings. Jim said we must get Miss Flannery, the assistant art teacher, down to have a look. Dolly Stewart would have been there at the time doing crafts with the women. Miss Flannery came down, and I remember feeling a very shy country boy. I think she was genuinely impressed with the quality of the drawings, and she encouraged me to start immediately. I came in and out by train for the first year. Tom Ryan was my first teacher, though he was also doing a bit of teaching in Dublin at the time. I recall Tom saying to me that nobody has painted since Sir Joshua Reynolds, and I mentioned Van Gogh and people like that. He dismissed them as daubers. That may be unfair to Tom, but that was the impression I got from him.

He was coming from an academic perspective.

Yes, a fine academic painter. Tom instructed me that I wasn't to paint for the first twelve months; instead I was to begin by drawing the antique statues. After a month I was fed up drawing Venus. I would go home from art school and paint at night. At that time in art school the only thing you could do was the ATC, the Art Teachers' Certificate. I wasn't terrible keen to be doing exams after my previous school experiences, but for the lack of something better to do I was entered for the exams.

I had been there a year when Pat McEvoy was appointed as headmaster. He was from Glasgow, but with an Irish background, very Irish really. He was talented, a good painter, a bit safe for my liking, but he had a very good understanding of the Impressionists and the Post-Impressionists. He knew what was going on in the 20th-century art world. That opened a whole world for me. What I found frustrating in the '50s was there was nobody I could talk to about painting until McEvoy arrived.

A sense that contemporary art did not exist in Limerick then?

Yes. Even in the 1960s I found Limerick like that. The contemporary art world did not feature, even for people like Phil Andrews, a very fine watercolourist, who looked after the picture gallery here at the [Carnegie] library [now Limerick City Gallery of Art]; and the Arts Club, who were a great old crowd and very proud of their academic tradition. They had produced [Seán] Keating, and Dermod O'Brien and Tom Ryan.

When did you begin teaching?

What happened was McEvoy came and insisted that I do more ATC exams, which I did and for which I got a few firsts and gold medals. I was doing the exams and Tom Ryan had a lot of teaching hours in St Gerard's and some in the art school, but he was also having exhibitions in Dublin. Michael Hayes, head of St Gerard's, would ring up McEvoy and say, 'For God's sake. There is a crowd of kids screaming here. Send down someone; send down young Donovan.' I was only eighteen or nineteen, and these fellows were as big as me; they were fifteen or sixteen.

If you survived St Gerard's you could survive anything. But they were great; it was just a case of entertaining them. Doing that was more or less how I was duped into teaching. Then hours came up in the art school itself. I was paid at a student rate.

Was it good money at the time?

Well my father did not leave me short, but it was good drinking money. I was corrupted early, you know. But I grew up in that culture. My father was a chronic alcoholic, but he would also work very hard. He was a binge-drinker, and then being a chemist, he could ease himself off. I swore I would never be like him, as with all children of alcoholics. However, within ten years of social drinking I was exactly like that. I always remember one day – I was married at the time – I was going to the races, and I called into the shop in Rathkeale. I asked him to cash a cheque, and as I was writing the cheque he spotted the shake in my hand and he said, 'You must have been at it hard. You have to give up the bloody stuff.' He would give me tablets to help me sleep, and I would stay dry for ten or twelve months at a time. It's amazing the ways you follow; I started the very same pattern as him. I have done that for the best part of my life.

When did you spend time in Edinburgh?

Pat McEvoy was from Edinburgh. We went for a few trips, the first during the Edinburgh Festival, and I recall seeing a very good Gauguin exhibition. From then on I went on summer courses, and through McEvoy I met some very good contemporary Scottish painters.

McEvoy was great in the sense that he opened up possibilities for me, but he was also limited. I can always remember in 1956 or '57, the first time I saw Jackson Pollock reproduced in colour in a magazine, and being very excited about it, bringing it in from Rathkeale and showing it to McEvoy and Mannering, his assistant, who was also Scots-Irish, and a very fine teacher. They more or less dismissed it. I felt very let down.

I often remember Pat McEvoy in his office talking politics with people like Seán South, who used to come up visiting the school at the time. McEvoy was always very political. He started this Christian Republican Party; the Fianna Fáil crowd were none too happy with him. He dragged us all into it for a while, making banners.

Returning to the Pollock, what did you see that they did not or could not see?

What I saw was something new, something that was not seen before, an abstract statement. I was so excited by these images. It suddenly dawned on me that I was on my own, there was nobody to share with. I suddenly, artistically or aesthetically, became alive, or matured. I think the year was 1957, I would have been 22 or 23 at the time, and it dawned on me: 'Look Jack, nobody can tell you what is good in art or what's bad. You have to follow your own way.' So I took responsibility for my own aestheticism.

When did you think you made a breakthrough in your work?

I was very frustrated until well into my thirties. I admired Bacon, Picasso and Velázquez. I loved all good painting. I felt my work was derivative of these artists.

Looking at the early 1960s works you exhibited in the Living Art exhibition, there is evidence of Bacon, or, rather, there is a confluence of styles and references.

Seeing some of the old stuff is like seeing ghosts from the past; some of these paintings I haven't seen in forty years. But what amazed me, particularly in the *Ballerinas* painting of 1961, is that I didn't realise I was using that black dot for the eyes so early.

Benedict Tutty used to say he saw me as the most Irish of Irish painters; he felt the paintings were coming right from the high crosses and the Ardagh chalice. It's very hard to know where your subject matter comes from. Certainly the stories I used to hear as a child had an influence. The Colleen Bawn was a famous murder out near us, and my grandmother's grandmother said she was at dances with the fellow that killed her, John Scanlon. Again there is the old Stewart thing – my great grandmother's people fought at the Boyne, and the family history has been explored. Also, during the war years, we had no other entertainment apart from storytelling. Later, we did have the cinema in Rathkeale and we had Duffy's circus, which was exciting as a child, and very frightening.

Where does the Balcony Series *come from?*

The only thing I can think of is that when, as a child, I was living with my grandmother in Grouse Lodge, looking out from the kitchen there was a very high half-door, almost like a stable door, and there were steps going up to it. In the evening, doing my homework in the kitchen over near the fire with one of the oil lamps, I could see the servant girl or the workmen coming in from the yard, and all you would see was the head cut off at the neck, almost, over the half-door, and I am convinced that this imagery is there surfacing in the work.

The nursery at Grouse Lodge is another subject you return to again and again. Does it hold special memories for you?

I remember a long room with a large press at the end. It was full of old bits and pieces: cricket bats, croquet sticks, dolls with their hair hanging down over their faces, one eye open, broken legs. These were old Victorian items from two generations previous, and they held a great fascination for me. My grandmother would let me look, but she was very precious about them. Looking in through that nursery doorway really excited me.

When I begin a painting I don't have a particular idea or theme. The title comes at the end when it dawns on me where the ideas have come from.

Why did you start using collage?

I suppose I was always interested in the female nude. I recall once, when I wanted a quick nude for my *Pinkie Downey* series, I did not want to paint it, and there were some old girlie magazines strewn around the place, so I found a nice reclining nude, and rather than going to the bother of painting, I cut it out and stuck it on. Then I did not like the head of the nude, so I decided to look through another magazine – it could have been

Woman's Own. There was a nicer head, but maybe a little too big for the scale, and it suddenly struck me this scale difference was exciting. It was distorting, but it wasn't distortion if I could get the balance right. I used collage all through the '60s and even into the late '70s for that reason. I could do things with this method: I cut up bits of bodies, bits of hands, and used them out of context, and it was exciting for me visually. There was nobody else doing it that particular way. Well, Picasso and Braque had used collage, but in a more formal manner, and that gave me confidence. Suddenly, by my early thirties, I could say that's a Jack Donovan and nobody else is painting like that.

You are not precious about your materials, like some painters.

Well, I started to use board because it was easier to stick the collage on. Likewise, I would use house paint if that was the colour I needed – Bacon did it too – and I would use anything to prepare my ground. There are no rules; I always objected to that idea in art school. Simply through trial and error, you find what works for you. Like with the collage in the '70s, it was an accident I jumped on and used.

You chose to remain in Limerick city.

I could have got a scholarship to Dublin; if you wanted to advance to do a diploma in painting you had to go to the National College. McEvoy, and he was dead right, said Keating will spoil you; he had no time for Keating, he talked me out of it. I was getting frustrated as I did not like teaching at the time – it was mainly secondary school and big night classes at the art school. When I first started showing work, McEvoy said I was too immature, but I showed in the Living Art from 1958 on.

My earliest memories of your work are in the 1970s, which featured the nudes using collage. But I also recall seeing religious figures in those paintings.

I had no personal issue with the church. I think a lot on both sides of my family were Church of Ireland. There was a lot of inter-church marriage around Rathkeale. The whole history of western art is saturated with religious imagery, of course.

Susannah and the Elders
1975-76, oil and collage on board, 129 x 190 cm

Poet and Family
1980, oil and collage on board, 99 x 92 cm (detail)

Monsignor's Garden
1996-00, oil on canvas, 124 x 94 cm (detail)
(Limerick City Gallery)y)

So you had no personal conflict with the church, but perhaps its dogma.

I always had a great curiosity and was an avid reader. There was a good library in Rathkeale, and I remember reading a Lutheran theologian who put forward the view that Jesus was first human and had brothers, James and John – he was part of a large family, perhaps the eldest. When I brought this up at school, I was put outside the door. And when I was about fourteen, I discovered Darwin, and it certainly dawned on me that our whole history of civilisation is based on a false premise.

Were you being deliberately provocative in the use of the nude images of women?

I don't think so.

The use of a nude female in relation to a clothed male has been problematic since Manet's Dejeuner sur l'herbe. *It's a subject or device that still creates a frisson, unease or transgression.*

Rather than sexuality, it has more to do with the aesthetics of flesh and the juxtaposition of black and white clothes. Maybe there is sexuality in there as well. The main reason would be a jolt for the eye rather than the penis, or maybe they go together, who knows? All I know is what excites me visually; sometimes it works, sometimes it does not.

So you regard yourself as a free-thinker, and the work is formalist, which is involved with the visual attractions that excite you.

We have always been obsessed by sex, and we are only here because of it. And if you are a heterosexual male, you are going to be fascinated by the female body, which, at its best, I would consider the most beautiful animal in the world. I don't believe in conventional morality. We are a crazy mixed-up species, and we have denied ourselves, and invented gods and spirituality. There is a need to be understood, loved, and everything else is pie in the sky.

Over your life, apart from your sense of man being very self-

destructive, can you describe your own sense of joy in aestheticism, your compulsion for painting.

I love life, I'm passionate about painting; it's the only thing I do reasonable well. It has been my life. Even bad painting, I enjoy.

One can detect angst or disengagement with society in the work, but also humanity and a love for aesthetics. There's a type of dualism.

Yes, that's why I have no time for pure abstraction. For me, as an artist, you must make some kind of comment on the human condition as you see it. I would hope to put forward my own personal idea of beauty, my own personal idea of aesthetics. If I don't fulfil that, it has failed.

You are a compulsive painter and you have created a unique body of work.

I don't think I have ever been fashionable. People will always want to paint, or sculpt or make imagery. It is part of our response to the human condition. To paraphrase Gerry Adams – painters haven't gone away, you know! One thing I can't stand is bad academic work which creates this kind of pictorialism. I have always maintained that all great figurative art is basically abstract. Just look at Velázquez.

I haven't alluded to your Pinkie Downey series, *named after a Limerick brothel, and to which, almost in a mythical way, your work is continuously linked.*

It may be. Funnily enough, Desmond O'Grady and myself knew some of the girls that worked there; they had a flat in Catherine Street. I think Pinkie's had burnt down, but really I was just looking for a title, not so much wishing to create a brothel scene but rather a setting for nudes on beds and black stuff.– material that is – again getting back to the excitement of flesh and black-and-white materials, which just interests me visually.

In terms of Limerick in the 1950s, did this work represent an alternative culture to the predominant conservatism?

If you wanted to be repressed in Limerick you certainly could be, but to me it was a very exciting place. On the surface, it was three nights a week walking to the Arch Confraternity. There was all that religious structure, but there were places in the docks, like the Crow's Nest, and I suppose you'd call it a gay bar before its time; and there were two pubs on the docks where you could pick up female company. Because it was so repressive there were always people at the other extreme.

You had another scene, with people like Kitty Bredin, who was very interested in the arts, particularly drama; the poet O'Grady before he moved to Paris; and Dickie Harris, before he went away. You had no university, so places like pubs, particularly the White House in the '60s, became a kind of intellectual centre.

You had the Seán South type of rosary-bead republican; however, there was also, even in my own family, those who believed in a secular, old French type of republicanism. McEvoy was a totally committed socialist and a total committed Catholic; he started the Christian Republican party, which I did not hold with. In any case, it was these politics that led to his departure.

You became principal of the art school then?

Well, by accident. McEvoy wanted to me to go back to Scotland with him. He said he could get me teaching in Edinburgh. I did not want to teach at all. I had married a national school teacher, and I thought I would paint, and maybe do a bit of part-time teaching. Yann Goulet was first choice and I heard I was second choice. I met a councillor and he informed me that I could end up running the art school. He told me the majority of the VEC did not want 'another bloody foreigner'. Goulet, it was said at the time, was under sentence of death in France for his Breton separatist activities, and conservative Limerick wanted one of their own. I ended up with a full-time job that I did not want. I was 28 at the time.

I recall hearing about a letter in the Limerick Leader, *complaining about you advertising for nude models, saying that you would be better off spending the money on Masses to save your soul.*

The Magician
1990/91, oil on canvas,
164 x 121 cm (detail)

After Velázquez
1978, oil and collage
on board, 122 x 86 cm
(detail)

It was very difficult to have a female model; in McEvoy's time they had to get permission from the bishop. I took over in 1962, and I said that I needed a female model. I went to the head of the VEC, and he said the bishop would not allow it. I said I had no interest in bishops, I needed a female model. The ad went in, and within a week we had a little lassie in from Shannon. She was down from the North with the Troubles, a lovely model.

I remember the week after Newman was made bishop, Mick Ryan, the principal of the secondary school below us in Mulgrave Street, rang me, and I probably had a hangover. He told me I was to be on my best behaviour as the bishop was coming. He enquired what was going on in the school that day; I said there was pottery. He asked would there be life-drawing, and I said of course, as the exams were in a month's time. 'Is it a male?' he asked. 'No, it's a female model, Yvonne.' 'Could you close it down for today?' he requested. 'I will in my arse close it down,' I replied, 'if he comes up, he comes up. If you don't want him to see it, you just pass the door.'

So how did the episcopal visit go?

I was painting a portrait at the time, as it was only during the day the sitter was available. It's a bloody awful painting; no wonder it was so bad. The first thing I saw was someone scurrying across the floor, going down on one knee and kissing Newman's ring. Then Mick Ryan came up, with Newman alongside, and asked would I show him around. First I took him down to Jim Dennison – I thought it was the safest place – and he and Val Dennison showed him the pottery. We next went to Ted Clifford, and we were coming up towards the life room, and Newman kept alongside me, so I had no choice when the bishop asked what was going on there. I said it's the life class. 'Oh, can I see it?' he asked. I said sure, and the boys behind went all quiet. I opened the door, and there was Yvonne, you know, in mid-pose; she was standing with a pole in her hand. In fairness to Bishop Newman, he did not bat an eyelid, but there were six nuns in their large habits gathered around, all drawing the model. I asked Yvonne to take to a rest, so she put her robe on. Newman went over and shook her hand, and asked where she was from. She told him about the Troubles and why she had moved down to Shannon. Then he talked to some of the nuns and they explained they had to do this exam to get their ATCs.

Newman did say afterwards, 'Was it really necessary to have nude models? Could Mr Donovan not use the antique statues?' They explained that it was a Department stipulation. What they did not know was that I had written the exams papers. I had put in that wherever possible a female model should be used.

What brought about the growth of the art school?

The art inspector Gerry de Brun brought in forward-looking regulations about teaching art, and soon people were calling me the Reverend Mother because of the number of nuns going through the school to complete the teaching exams. Then middle-class parents realised there were jobs in teaching, and if their son or daughter had a bit of talent they would let them go to art school. As the school grew in the 1970s, I was asked to stand down as head and I was delighted. I still used to do the student registers, and I always had time for painting.

Now that you are retired from teaching you are painting perhaps even more than ever, and the work has changed again.

I don't know. I have two styles of working – a classic or simple style, and then a more Rococo style, and I oscillate and react against myself between these two.

Looking back at your paintings over the years, what strikes you about the work now?

Seeing this one, *After Velázquez,* amazed me. It's so alive after all that time; this one gives me a buzz. I remember there was another one completed at the time, a balcony scene. But it fell off the roof-rack of the car and smashed. At times you wonder why you did not do more of those types of works, but visually we bore very quickly. It is impossible to predict what you will be doing in two weeks' time.

Mike Fitzpatrick is Director / Curator of Limerick City Gallery of Art.

Limerick at night
1959, oil on canvas, 40 x 29 cm

Nude drying her hair 1962-63, oil on board, 102 x 102 cm

Nude turning over   1962-63, oil on board, 122 x 122 cm

Ballerinas
1961, oil on board, 79 x 59 cm

Gerard Ryan
1971, pen and pencil on paper, 29 x 24 cm
(National Collection of Contemporary Drawing, LCGA)

Old Woman Reading
1973, mixed media on paper, 30 x 23 cm (detail)
(National Collection of Contemporary Drawing, LCGA)

The Pilgrim
1971, oil and collage
on board, 93 x 84 cm

The Old Canon
1973, mixed media and collage on paper, 20 x 23 cm

Laughing Girl
1974, paint and collage on paper, 30 x 23 cm

Kitty Bredin
early 1970s, oil on board, 60 x 50 cm (detail)
(Limerick City Gallery of Art)

The Poet Ryan
1973, oil on board, 122 x 91.5 cm
(Limerick City Gallery of Art)

Wedding Series
c.1975, oil and collage on board,
78 x 60 cm

Susannah and the Elders
1975-76, oil and collage on board, 129 x 190 cm

Untitled (nude with seated figure)
1976, oil and collage on board, 54 x 40 cm

opposite
Balcony Series (with self-portrait)
1978, oil and collage on board, 75 x 70 cm

30

Portrait of Mary Nagle
1977/78, oil on board, 61 x 46 cm

After Velázquez
1978, oil and collage on board, 122 x 86 cm

Woman seated on bed (originally *Pinkie Downey's Slip*)
1979, oil and collage on board, 60 x 52 cm

Richard III
1980-81, oil and collage on board, 60 x 44 cm (approx)

After the Ball
1980, oil on board,
66 x 56 cm

Woman on couch
1980-84, oil on board, 92 x 92 cm
(Mary Immaculate College, University of Limerick)

opposite
Poet and Family
1980, oil and collage on board, 99 x 92 cm

Kilkee III
1995, oil on board, 84 x 78 cm

opposite
Kilkee I
1987, oil on canvas, 120 x 90 cm

Kilkee – Clown on beach
1991, oil on canvas, 85 x 76 cm

Sarsfield's farewell to Limerick
1984, oil on canvas, 92 x 92 cm

Pinkie Downey on couch
1987/88, oil and collage on board, 92 x 76 cm

Croom of the Merriment
1990-96, oil on canvas,
125 x 104 cm

opposite
In the Garden
1988/89, oil on board,
122 x 122 cm

St George and the Dragon
1990, oil and collage on board, 78 x 60 cm

Circus Clown and Nude
1989, oil on board, 122 x 122 cm

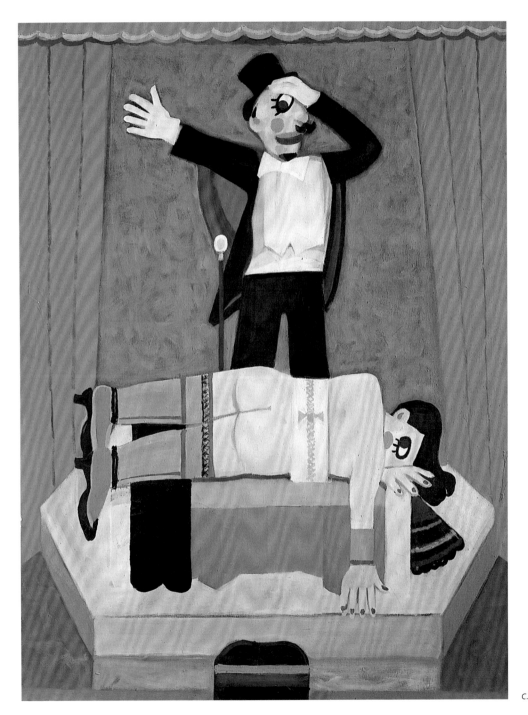

The Magician
c.1990/91, oil on canvas, 164 x 121 cm

The Madam – Pinkie Downey series
1994, oil on canvas, 129 x 105 cm

Bottoms Up – Pinkie Downey series
1994, oil on canvas, 105 x 94 cm (detail)

Clown and Ring
1998/99, oil on board, 61 x 61 cm

opposite
The Nursery, Grouse Lodge
1993/94, oil on board, 123 x 105 cm

Dane in Kenry
1995/96, oil on board, 60 x 60 cm

Crucifixion with Two Donors III
1997/98, oil on board, 70 x 60 cm

Monsignor's Garden
1996-2000, oil on canvas, 124 x 94 cm
(Limerick City Gallery of Art)

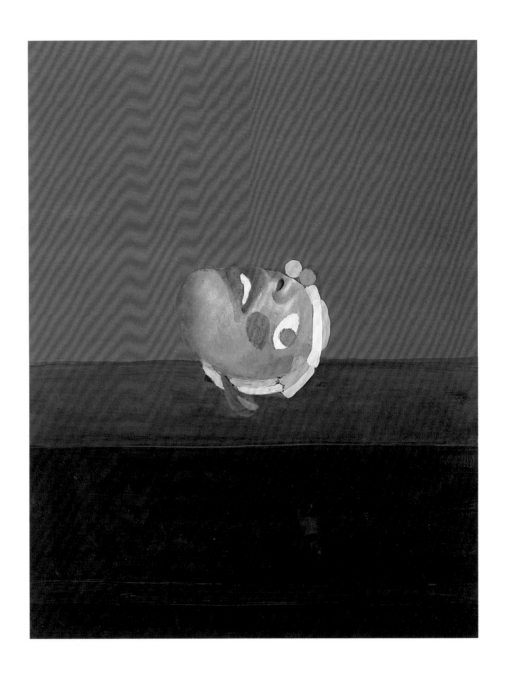

The Head of Princess Orlaith
1999/2000, oil and collage on board, 70 x 55 cm
(Limerick City Gallery of Art)

Detail from a Siege
2001, oil on board, 89 x 79 cm

53

Ringmaster
2002/03, oil on board, 49 x 49 cm

opposite
Death of Mahon
2000, oil on board, 92 x 78 cm

Clown with pink elephant
2002, oil on board, 84 x 79 cm

Poet and Muse
2002, oil on board, 89 x 79 cm

Othello III
1999/2000, oil on board, 71 x 63 cm

Nude with a kite
2003, oil on board, 75 x 70 cm

The Nursery, Grouse Lodge
2003, oil on board, 90 x 78 cm

Three Graces with Dachshund
2004, oil on board, 89 x 80 cm

opposite
Temptation of Saint Anthony
2003, oil on board, 89 x 80 cm

Annunciation
2003, oil on board, 72 x 61 cm

Flowers in red jug, blue background
2003, oil on board, 41 x 32 cm

Flowers in gravy dish
2002, oil on board, 41 x 32 cm

top
Clown, ring and bowler
2003, oil on board, 51 x 41 cm

bottom left
Clown ringmaster
2003, oil on board, 79 x 71 cm

Clown seated
2004, oil on board, 79 x 71 cm

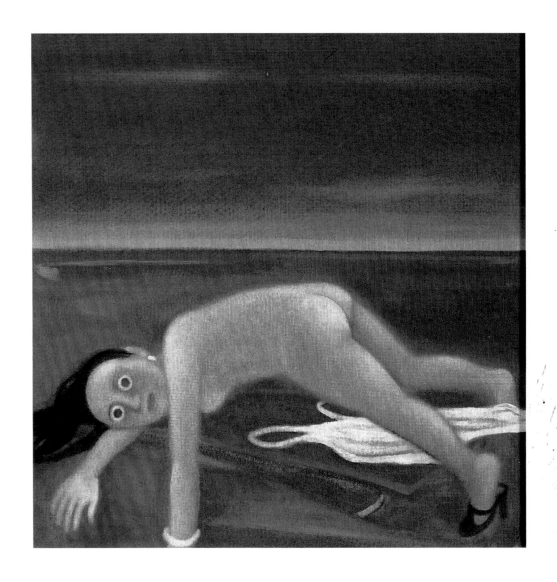

Colleen Bawn with one shoe
2003, oil on board, 79 x 79 cm

Nursery – Pinkie Downey series
2003, oil on board, 80 x 70 cm

The head of Staker Wallace
2003, oil on board, 76 x 60 cm (detail)

opposite
Couple on balcony with balloon
2003-04, oil and collage on board, 81 x 66 cm

Head of Turloch O'Brien
2003, oil on board, 56 x 61 cm

Leo of Tullavine
2003, oil on board, 81 x 66 cm

opposite
Ballyneety II
2002-03, oil on board, 81 x 76 cm

Young Pretender with two companions
2003-04, oil on board, 81 x 66 cm

Bishop's Lady
2003, oil on board, 81 x 66 cm

Susannah and the Elders
2004, oil on board, 94 x 84 cm

Trapeze – Circus series
2004, oil and collage on board, 84 x 79 cm

Nude, Pony and Clown
2004, oil on board, 84 x 80 cm

Donovan
A Question of Balance

JOHN SHINNORS

SITTING IN THE WHITE HOUSE BAR IN LIMERICK SOME TIME AGO WITH JACK DONOVAN, IT occurred to me that I have known him for as long as I have been frequenting the White House; this has been the best part of thirty-five years. The White House bar has always been, and remains to this day, a popular meeting place for actors, poets, musicians and artists, and, as in many establishments of its type, it's not unusual to see photographs of the famous and not-so-famous adorn its walls. Some are still with us, and remain actively involved in the arts; others known to us have passed on. Pointing to a photograph of one painter-friend in particular, now deceased, I remark to Donovan that I have never understood why he was buried in Mungret (a village in Co Limerick; our friend was a city man). Donovan muses silently for a moment, meditatively nodding, before replying: 'Well, because he was dead I suppose.'

I do not attempt to follow that particular line of conversation any further, and return to our talk of painting and his recent one-man show in the Cross Gallery. He appears to be happy with the show: 'It looked well, it had the balance.' Pitch of balance is an important preoccupation in Donovan's work, and is a favourite expression of his when describing his work.

Self-Portrait
2003, oil on canvas, 58 x 53 cm

Our talk moves to the past. Of the many paintings I admire by Donovan, a particular favourite springs to mind, *The Barber and his Wife on Vacation*. I ask him does he know of its whereabouts. He is not exactly sure; after all, it is three decades since he created that painting. I inquire if there is a photograph or some other recorded reproduction; the unsurprising answer is no. Back in the late sixties, early seventies, most artists were not in any great rush to have everything they did recorded. The age of the glossy individual artist's catalogue was a rare thing, and the 'career artist' was practically unheard of in this country.

The Barber and his Wife on Vacation (presuming it still exists) is a medium-sized oil collage. I first saw this painting in the old Limerick School of Art, when I entered as a seventeen-year-old student. The title of the work describes exactly the image of the painting – the figures of a man and woman, with all the usual holiday trappings, standing on a deserted beach – and, although a modern painting, it had all the solid, earthy richness of a seventeenth-century Dutch painting and a mysterious Rubenesque luminosity, all compacted into one coherent, balanced image.

Donovan will tell you that he is an image-maker. He will speak of European schools, of which he is very well informed, and their influences on his work, although the only place outside of Ireland he has been is England. This aspect of the man, knowing him as I do, is not surprising. Donovan is that breed of artist who sees the universal in the local. The complex, the mysterious, the banal and the simple are uncovered in life as he lives and experiences it here on this small rock on the edge of Europe. *The Barber* to my youthful eyes had all the ingredients of Classicism, high Baroque and the 'new', and had a profound and mesmeric effect on me, which has not left me to this day.

The reason I asked him about the location of the work is because Mike Fitzpatrick (the director of Limerick City Gallery of Art) asked if I could be of help in locating early work by Donovan for the retrospective exhibition. The last major showing of Donovan's work was at the same gallery some twenty years ago, when the gallery was a small area at the back of Carnegie Library.

The Limerick School of Art, when I first studied there, was situated on the top floor of what was originally the County Hospital. One could feel Donovan's presence almost immediately. Some of his paintings hung on the walls of the corridor in a haphazard way, almost as if they had been abandoned. I remember seeing him stand before one of these paintings, scrutinising it intently, then go to his painting place and return with a loaded paintbrush, and with a few deft flicks, correct the area he was dissatisfied with and return to where he had come from.

I was fortunate to be with him where he painted, on more than one occasion, on that wide corridor on the other side of the school. Once I observed he had been working on a series of five paintings. I asked him (not knowing any better at the time) if he had a favourite. This is like asking a parent if they have a favourite child. He paused for a moment, and pointing to a painting he had completed, enigmatically replied, 'That one painted itself.'

To me and my fellow students, Donovan was an artist who practised his art almost with us. His self-imposed presence was unique and, even in those heady days, unorthodox. The area at the far side of the school was his studio. He was oblivious to the system – banging doors, raucous students, etc, a situation other artists would find intolerable. For Donovan, the buzzing life of people about him was never a distraction; for this easy-going and nonchalant painter-tutor, being called to the phone was the only time when he would seem to get irritated.

As I got to know him and understand him better, I noticed that with students he believed would become painters, he would freely impart information and knowledge, and share with them his enthusiasm and love for painting. There was about him then, as there is now, a mixture of generosity of spirit and inherited ould decency. I have never heard him bitch or sneer about other painters, amateur or professional; this would be beneath him. Nor do I ever remember him trying to impress anyone. His love for painting is matched only by the attention given to his beloved garden. As with the works which hung almost abandoned in the school until they needed that extra touch, so his home is filled with works in progress; his studio

Untitled (nude with seated figure)
1976, oil and collage on board, 54 x 40 cm
(detail)

Ballyneety II
2002-03, oil on board, 81 x 76 cm (detail)

Colleen Bawn with one shoe
2003, oil on board, 79 x 79 cm

seems to be everywhere, sometimes even running into the garden itself.

Donovan continues to work as the work calls him. I recall one discussion about painting at his home recently – returning to the topic of the European influences – asking why he never went to brighter, sunnier climes. His reply was slow and simply put: 'That light is for certain painters. I mean, I paint with one candle. Painting for me is about ideas. I was never that kind of painter; painting was always about saying something, saying something that meant something to me. Painting should be visual poetry really. You know, you paint the things you love, the things you imagine. A lot of my imagery comes from my childhood: Duffy's Circus, the cinema, Anew McMaster, the old plays in the hall at Rathkeale. It's the things that excite you as a child, and your own ideas, like my own history of the Stuarts, my Sieges of Limerick. That's what excites me.'

The quote is as much as Donovan will be drawn on his own work. But over the course of my friendship with him, I have seen paintings that have spoken of much more, the childhood memory of circus being put to a darker and more serious exposition than Donovan's explanation would belie. Even where the image is quite clear, the balance between what is seen and said creates a peculiar tension within the work. It is in this quality of balanced tension the painting reveals itself, and it's not always a happy story. Donovan's work can be, by turns, political, acerbic, witty, satiric, and often humorous. The balance of the image with what is being said is all-important in achieving the statement of the painting.

John Shinnors is an artist who lives and works in Limerick. His work has been published in *Profile 18 – John Shinnors* (Gandon Editions, 2002) and *John Shinnors – Paintings and Drawings* (LCGA / Gandon, 2002).

An earlier version of this article appeared as an illustrated feature in *Irish Arts Review*, winter 2003.

LIST OF ILLUSTRATIONS

dimensions in centimetres – height x width

Con Kelleher

JACK DONOVAN

1934   Born in Limerick
1951   Began studies at Limerick School of Art
1962-78   Head of Limerick School of Art
1996   Retired from teaching at Limerick School of Art
    Lives and works in Limerick

SOLO EXHIBITIONS

2005   *A Selection from the Retrospective*, West Cork Arts Centre, Skibbereen; Draíocht Arts Centre, Blanchardstown
2004   *Retrospective of Paintings 1959-2004*, Limerick City Gallery of Art
2003   Cross Gallery, Dublin
    Moulin Gallery, Limerick
1993   Wyvern Gallery, Dublin
1991   Wyvern Gallery, Dublin
1988   Taylor Galleries, Dublin
1985   *Retrospective*, Limerick City Gallery of Art
1977   Belltable Arts Centre, Limerick
1977   Cummins Gallery, Limerick
1976   Emmet Gallery, Dublin
1964   Dublin Painters Gallery

SELECTED GROUP EXHIBITIONS

2001   *As I See Myself – reflections of Limerick artists through their self-portraits and work*, Hunt Museum, Limerick
1998   *Jack Donovan, John Shinnors, Richard Slade*, Belltable Arts Centre, Limerick
1994   *Recent Works*, Vangard Gallery, Macroom (with Henry Morgan)

1992   *Jack Donovan, John Shinnors*, Riverrun Gallery, Galway
1990   *Donovan, Morgan, Shinnors – Recent Paintings*, Limerick City Gallery of Art
1989   *National Self-Portrait Collection*, Belfast, Dublin
1983   *EV⁺A 83*, Limerick
1980   *EV⁺A 80*, Limerick
1979   *EV⁺A 79*, Limerick
1971   *Rosc '71 – Young Irish Artists*, Galway
1958-80   showed regularly at Irish Exhibition of Living Art, Dublin

PUBLIC COLLECTIONS

An Chomhairle Ealaíon / The Arts Council; Arts Council of Northern Ireland; Arts Council of Great Britain; CIÉ; Limerick City Gallery of Art; National Self-Portrait Collection of Ireland; Swedish Academy of Visual Art

BIBLIOGRAPHY

2004   *Jack Donovan: Retrospective of Paintings 1959-2004* (Limerick City Gallery of Art); published in paperback as *Profile 19 – Jack Donovan* (Gandon Editions)
2003   *The Song of Songs*, a version by Desmond O'Grady, illustrations by Jack Donovan (Anam Press, Kinsale)
    John Shinnors, 'Donovan – A Question of Balance', *Irish Arts Review*, winter, 82-87
1990   *Donovan Morgan Shinnors – Recent Paintings*, essay by Gerry Dukes (Limerick City Gallery of Art)
1982   Roderic Knowles, 'Jack Donovan: A Sensualist View' in *Contemporary Irish Art* (Wolfhound Press, Dublin)

GANDON EDITIONS

Gandon Editions is the leading producer of books on Irish art and architecture. Established in 1983, it was named after the architect James Gandon (1743-1823) as the initial focus was on architecture titles. We now produce 20 art and architecture titles per year, both under the Gandon imprint and on behalf of a wide range of art and architectural institutions in Ireland. We have produced over 280 titles to date. Gandon books are available from good bookshops in Ireland and abroad, or direct from Gandon Editions.

PROFILES

In 1996, Gandon Editions launched PROFILES – a series of medium-format books on contemporary Irish artists. In 1997, we launched ARCHITECTURE PROFILES – a companion series on contemporary Irish architects. Both series are edited and designed by John O'Regan.

Each volume in the PROFILES series carries at least two major texts – a critical essay and an interview with the artist or architect – and is comprehensively illustrated in colour. In response to demand from readers, we have expanded the pagination and colour content of both series, reinforcing the two PROFILES series as the key reference series on contemporary Irish art and architecture.

Profile 1 – PAULINE FLYNN
essays by Paul M O'Reilly and Gus Gibney
ISBN 0946641 722   Gandon Editions, 1996
48 pages   22 illus (incl 19 col)   €10 pb

Profile 2 – SEÁN McSWEENEY
essay by Brian Fallon; interview by Aidan Dunne
ISBN 0946641 862   Gandon, Winter 2004
(2nd revised and expanded ed; 1st ed, 1996)
60 pages   col illus   €10 pb

Profile 3 – EILÍS O'CONNELL
essay by Caoimhín Mac Giolla Léith; interview by
Medb Ruane
ISBN 0946641 870   Gandon Editions, 1997
48 pages   35 illus (incl 27 col)   €10 pb

Profile 4 – SIOBÁN PIERCY
essay by Aidan Dunne; interview by Vera Ryan
ISBN 0946641 900   Gandon Editions, 1997
48 pages   38 illus (incl 32 col)   €10 pb

Profile 5 – MARY LOHAN
essay by Noel Sheridan; intro and interview by
Aidan Dunne
ISBN 0946641 889   Gandon Editions, 1998
48 pages   22 illus (incl 21 col)   €10 pb

Profile 6 – ALICE MAHER
essay and interview by Medb Ruane
ISBN 0946641 935   Gandon Editions, 1998
48 pages   29 illus (incl 23 col)   €10 pb

Profile 7 – CHARLES HARPER
essay by Gerry Walker; interview by Aidan
Dunne; afterword by Bob Baker
ISBN 0946846 111   Gandon Editions, 1998
48 pages   24 illus (incl 19 col)   €10 pb

Profile 8 – MAUD COTTER
essay and interview by Luke Clancy
ISBN 0946846 073   Gandon Editions, 1998
48 pages   30 illus (incl 24 col)   €10 pb

Profile 9 – MICHEAL FARRELL
essay by Aidan Dunne; intro and interview by
Gerry Walker
ISBN 0946846 138   Gandon Editions, 1998
48 pages   33 illus (incl 25 col)   €10 pb

Profile 10 – BARRIE COOKE
intro by Seamus Heaney; essay by Aidan Dunne;
interview by Niall MacMonagle
ISBN 0946846 170   Gandon Editions, 1998
48 pages   29 illus (incl 25 col)   €10 pb

Profile 11 – VIVIENNE ROCHE
essay by Ciarán Benson; intro and interview by
Aidan Dunne
ISBN 0946846 235   Gandon Editions, 1999
48 pages   39 illus (incl 30 col)   €10 pb

Profile 12 – JAMES SCANLON
essay by Aidan Dunne; interview by Shane
O'Toole; afterword by Mark Patrick Hederman
ISBN 0946641 579   Gandon Editions, 2000
48 pages   51 illus (incl 37 col)   €10 pb

Profile 13 – TONY O'MALLEY
essay by Peter Murray; intros by Jay Gates, Jean
Kennedy Smith
ISBN 0946846 456   Gandon Editions, 2000
48 pages   30 illus (incl 26 col)   €10 pb

Profile 14 – ANDREW KEARNEY
essay by Simon Ofield; interview by Aoife
Mac Namara, intro by Mike Fitzpatrick
ISBN 0946846 74X   Gandon Editions, 2001
60 pages   83 illus (incl 69 col)   €10 pb

Profile 15 – BERNADETTE KIELY
essay by Aidan Dunne; interview by Jo Allen;
afterword by Ciarán Benson
ISBN 0946846 804   Gandon Editions, 2002
60 pages   41 illus (incl 35 col)   €10 pb

Profile 16 – ANNE MADDEN
essay and interview by Aidan Dunne
ISBN 0946846 863   Gandon Editions, 2002
60 pages   42 illus (incl 37 col)   €10 pb

Profile 17 – ANDREW FOLAN
essay by Paul O'Brien; intro and interview by
Patrick T Murphy
ISBN 0946641 919   Gandon Editions, 2002
60 pages   57 illus (incl 46 col)   €10 pb

Profile 18 – JOHN SHINNORS
essay by Brian Fallon; intro and interview by
Aidan Dunne
ISBN 0946846 782   Gandon Editions, 2002
60 pages   51 illus (incl 49 col)   €10 pb

Profile 19 – JACK DONOVAN
essays by Gerry Dukes, Aidan Dunne, John
Shinnors; interview by Mike Fitzpatrick
ISBN 0946846 200   Gandon Editions, 2004
84 pages   90 illus (incl 71 col)   €15 pb

Profile 20 – TOM FITZGERALD
essay by Suzanne O'Shea, Seán Ó Laoire;
interview by Jim Savage
ISBN 0946846 618   Gandon Editions, 2004
84 pages   col illus   €15 pb

titles in preparation: Louis LE BROCQUY, Michael
CULLEN, Camille SOUTER, Daphne WRIGHT

ARCHITECTURE PROFILES

Profile 1 – O'DONNELL + TUOMEY
interview by Kester Rattenbury; texts by Hugh
Campbell, Kevin Kieran, Robert Maxwell, Wilfried
Wang, Williams & Tsien
ISBN 0946641 986   Gandon Editions, 1997
48 pages   64 illus (incl 27 col)   €10 pb

Profile 2 – McGARRY NíÉANAIGH
essay by Raymund Ryan; interview by
Dermot Boyd
ISBN 0946641 994   Gandon Editions, 1997
48 pages   56 illus (incl 26 col)   €10 pb

Profile 3 – GRAFTON ARCHITECTS
essays by Hugh Campbell, Kenneth Frampton,
Elizabeth Hatz; interview by Raymund Ryan
ISBN 0946846 057   Gandon Editions, 1999
60 pages   131 illus (incl 86 col)   €10 pb

Profile 4 – SHAY CLEARY
essay by Raymund Ryan; interview by Simon
Walker; afterword by Edward Jones
ISBN 0946846 898   Gandon Editions, 2002
132 pages   full-colour   320 illus   €20 pb